Child Daycare Log In/Out

Date: _______________________

Child's Name	Emergency Phone Number	Contact Name	Time In / Time Out	Signature

Child Daycare Log In/Out

Date: _______________________

Child's Name	Emergency Phone Number	Contact Name	Time In / Time Out	Signature

Child Daycare Log In/Out

Date: _________________________

Child's Name	Emergency Phone Number	Contact Name	Time In / Time Out	Signature

Child Daycare Log In/Out

Date: _______________________

Child's Name	Emergency Phone Number	Contact Name	Time In / Time Out	Signature

Child Daycare Log In/Out

Date: _________________________

Child's Name	Emergency Phone Number	Contact Name	Time In / Time Out	Signature

Child Daycare Log In/Out

Date: ________________________

Child's Name	Emergency Phone Number	Contact Name	Time In / Time Out	Signature

Child Daycare Log In/Out

Date: _______________________

Child's Name	Emergency Phone Number	Contact Name	Time In / Time Out	Signature

Child Daycare Log In/Out

Date: _________________________

Child's Name	Emergency Phone Number	Contact Name	Time In / Time Out	Signature

Child Daycare Log In/Out

Date: _______________________

Child's Name	Emergency Phone Number	Contact Name	Time In / Time Out	Signature

Child Daycare Log In/Out

Date: _______________________

Child's Name	Emergency Phone Number	Contact Name	Time In / Time Out	Signature

Child Daycare Log In/Out

Date: _______________________

Child's Name	Emergency Phone Number	Contact Name	Time In / Time Out	Signature

Child Daycare Log In/Out

Date: _________________

Child's Name	Emergency Phone Number	Contact Name	Time In / Time Out	Signature

Child Daycare Log In/Out

Date: ________________________

Child's Name	Emergency Phone Number	Contact Name	Time In / Time Out	Signature

Child Daycare Log In/Out

Date: _______________________

Child's Name	Emergency Phone Number	Contact Name	Time In / Time Out	Signature

Child Daycare Log In/Out

Date: _______________________

Child's Name	Emergency Phone Number	Contact Name	Time In / Time Out	Signature

Child Daycare Log In/Out

Date: _________________________

Child's Name	Emergency Phone Number	Contact Name	Time In / Time Out	Signature

Child Daycare Log In/Out

Date: _______________________

Child's Name	Emergency Phone Number	Contact Name	Time In / Time Out	Signature

Child Daycare Log In/Out

Date: _______________________

Child's Name	Emergency Phone Number	Contact Name	Time In / Time Out	Signature

Child Daycare Log In/Out

Date: _______________________

Child's Name	Emergency Phone Number	Contact Name	Time In / Time Out	Signature

Child Daycare Log In/Out

Date: _______________________

Child's Name	Emergency Phone Number	Contact Name	Time In / Time Out	Signature

Child Daycare Log In/Out

Date: _______________________

Child's Name	Emergency Phone Number	Contact Name	Time In / Time Out	Signature

Child Daycare Log In/Out

Date: _______________________

Child's Name	Emergency Phone Number	Contact Name	Time In / Time Out	Signature

Child Daycare Log In/Out

Date: _______________________

Child's Name	Emergency Phone Number	Contact Name	Time In / Time Out	Signature

Child Daycare Log In/Out

Date: _______________________

Child's Name	Emergency Phone Number	Contact Name	Time In / Time Out	Signature

Child Daycare Log In/Out

Date: _______________________

Child's Name	Emergency Phone Number	Contact Name	Time In / Time Out	Signature

Child Daycare Log In/Out

Date: ___________________

Child's Name	Emergency Phone Number	Contact Name	Time In / Time Out	Signature

Child Daycare Log In/Out

Date: ______________________

Child's Name	Emergency Phone Number	Contact Name	Time In / Time Out	Signature

Child Daycare Log In/Out

Date: _______________________

Child's Name	Emergency Phone Number	Contact Name	Time In / Time Out	Signature

Child Daycare Log In/Out

Date: _______________________

Child's Name	Emergency Phone Number	Contact Name	Time In / Time Out	Signature

Child Daycare Log In/Out

Date: ___________________

Child's Name	Emergency Phone Number	Contact Name	Time In / Time Out	Signature

Child Daycare Log In/Out

Date: _______________________

Child's Name	Emergency Phone Number	Contact Name	Time In / Time Out	Signature

Child Daycare Log In/Out

Date: _______________________

Child's Name	Emergency Phone Number	Contact Name	Time In / Time Out	Signature

Child Daycare Log In/Out

Date: _______________________

Child's Name	Emergency Phone Number	Contact Name	Time In / Time Out	Signature

Child Daycare Log In/Out

Date: _______________________

Child's Name	Emergency Phone Number	Contact Name	Time In / Time Out	Signature

Child Daycare Log In/Out

Date: _______________________

Child's Name	Emergency Phone Number	Contact Name	Time In / Time Out	Signature

Child Daycare Log In/Out

Date: _______________________

Child's Name	Emergency Phone Number	Contact Name	Time In / Time Out	Signature

Child Daycare Log In/Out

Date: _______________________

Child's Name	Emergency Phone Number	Contact Name	Time In / Time Out	Signature

Child Daycare Log In/Out

Date: _______________________

Child's Name	Emergency Phone Number	Contact Name	Time In / Time Out	Signature

Child Daycare Log In/Out

Date: _______________________

Child's Name	Emergency Phone Number	Contact Name	Time In / Time Out	Signature

Child Daycare Log In/Out

Date: _______________________

Child's Name	Emergency Phone Number	Contact Name	Time In / Time Out	Signature

Child Daycare Log In/Out

Date: _______________________

Child's Name	Emergency Phone Number	Contact Name	Time In / Time Out	Signature

Child Daycare Log In/Out

Date: _______________________

Child's Name	Emergency Phone Number	Contact Name	Time In / Time Out	Signature

Child Daycare Log In/Out

Date: _______________________

Child's Name	Emergency Phone Number	Contact Name	Time In / Time Out	Signature

Child Daycare Log In/Out

Date: ________________________

Child's Name	Emergency Phone Number	Contact Name	Time In / Time Out	Signature

Child Daycare Log In/Out

Date: ______________________

Child's Name	Emergency Phone Number	Contact Name	Time In / Time Out	Signature

Child Daycare Log In/Out

Date: _______________________

Child's Name	Emergency Phone Number	Contact Name	Time In / Time Out	Signature

Child Daycare Log In/Out

Date: _______________________

Child's Name	Emergency Phone Number	Contact Name	Time In / Time Out	Signature

Child Daycare Log In/Out

Date: _______________________

Child's Name	Emergency Phone Number	Contact Name	Time In / Time Out	Signature

Child Daycare Log In/Out

Date: _______________________

Child's Name	Emergency Phone Number	Contact Name	Time In / Time Out	Signature

Child Daycare Log In/Out

Date: _______________________

Child's Name	Emergency Phone Number	Contact Name	Time In / Time Out	Signature

Child Daycare Log In/Out

Date: _________________________

Child's Name	Emergency Phone Number	Contact Name	Time In / Time Out	Signature

Child Daycare Log In/Out

Date: _______________________

Child's Name	Emergency Phone Number	Contact Name	Time In / Time Out	Signature

Child Daycare Log In/Out

Date: _______________________

Child's Name	Emergency Phone Number	Contact Name	Time In / Time Out	Signature

Child Daycare Log In/Out

Date: _______________________

Child's Name	Emergency Phone Number	Contact Name	Time In / Time Out	Signature

Child Daycare Log In/Out

Date: _______________________

Child's Name	Emergency Phone Number	Contact Name	Time In / Time Out	Signature

Child Daycare Log In/Out

Date: ________________________

Child's Name	Emergency Phone Number	Contact Name	Time In / Time Out	Signature

Child Daycare Log In/Out

Date: _____________________

Child's Name	Emergency Phone Number	Contact Name	Time In / Time Out	Signature

Child Daycare Log In/Out

Date: _________________________

Child's Name	Emergency Phone Number	Contact Name	Time In / Time Out	Signature

Child Daycare Log In/Out

Date: _________________________

Child's Name	Emergency Phone Number	Contact Name	Time In / Time Out	Signature

Child Daycare Log In/Out

Date: _______________________

Child's Name	Emergency Phone Number	Contact Name	Time In / Time Out	Signature

Child Daycare Log In/Out

Date: _______________________

Child's Name	Emergency Phone Number	Contact Name	Time In / Time Out	Signature

Child Daycare Log In/Out

Date: _______________________

Child's Name	Emergency Phone Number	Contact Name	Time In / Time Out	Signature

Child Daycare Log In/Out

Date: _________________________

Child's Name	Emergency Phone Number	Contact Name	Time In / Time Out	Signature

Child Daycare Log In/Out

Date: _______________________

Child's Name	Emergency Phone Number	Contact Name	Time In / Time Out	Signature

Child Daycare Log In/Out

Date: _______________________

Child's Name	Emergency Phone Number	Contact Name	Time In / Time Out	Signature

Child Daycare Log In/Out

Date: _______________________

Child's Name	Emergency Phone Number	Contact Name	Time In / Time Out	Signature

Child Daycare Log In/Out

Date: _________________________

Child's Name	Emergency Phone Number	Contact Name	Time In / Time Out	Signature

Child Daycare Log In/Out

Date: _______________________

Child's Name	Emergency Phone Number	Contact Name	Time In / Time Out	Signature

Child Daycare Log In/Out

Date: ___________________

Child's Name	Emergency Phone Number	Contact Name	Time In / Time Out	Signature

Child Daycare Log In/Out

Date: _______________________

Child's Name	Emergency Phone Number	Contact Name	Time In / Time Out	Signature

Child Daycare Log In/Out

Date: _______________________

Child's Name	Emergency Phone Number	Contact Name	Time In / Time Out	Signature

Child Daycare Log In/Out

Date: _______________________

Child's Name	Emergency Phone Number	Contact Name	Time In / Time Out	Signature

Child Daycare Log In/Out

Date: _______________________

Child's Name	Emergency Phone Number	Contact Name	Time In / Time Out	Signature

Child Daycare Log In/Out

Date: _______________________

Child's Name	Emergency Phone Number	Contact Name	Time In / Time Out	Signature

Child Daycare Log In/Out

Date: _________________________

Child's Name	Emergency Phone Number	Contact Name	Time In / Time Out	Signature

Child Daycare Log In/Out

Date: _______________________

Child's Name	Emergency Phone Number	Contact Name	Time In / Time Out	Signature

Child Daycare Log In/Out

Date: _______________________

Child's Name	Emergency Phone Number	Contact Name	Time In / Time Out	Signature

Child Daycare Log In/Out

Date: _________________

Child's Name	Emergency Phone Number	Contact Name	Time In / Time Out	Signature

Child Daycare Log In/Out

Date: _______________________

Child's Name	Emergency Phone Number	Contact Name	Time In / Time Out	Signature

Child Daycare Log In/Out

Date: _______________________

Child's Name	Emergency Phone Number	Contact Name	Time In / Time Out	Signature

Child Daycare Log In/Out

Date: _______________________

Child's Name	Emergency Phone Number	Contact Name	Time In / Time Out	Signature

Child Daycare Log In/Out

Date: _______________________

Child's Name	Emergency Phone Number	Contact Name	Time In / Time Out	Signature

Child Daycare Log In/Out

Date: _____________________

Child's Name	Emergency Phone Number	Contact Name	Time In / Time Out	Signature

Child Daycare Log In/Out

Date: _______________________

Child's Name	Emergency Phone Number	Contact Name	Time In / Time Out	Signature

Child Daycare Log In/Out

Date: _______________________

Child's Name	Emergency Phone Number	Contact Name	Time In / Time Out	Signature

Child Daycare Log In/Out

Date: _______________________

Child's Name	Emergency Phone Number	Contact Name	Time In / Time Out	Signature

Child Daycare Log In/Out

Date: ___________________

Child's Name	Emergency Phone Number	Contact Name	Time In / Time Out	Signature

Child Daycare Log In/Out

Date: ________________________

Child's Name	Emergency Phone Number	Contact Name	Time In / Time Out	Signature

Child Daycare Log In/Out

Date: _______________________

Child's Name	Emergency Phone Number	Contact Name	Time In / Time Out	Signature

Child Daycare Log In/Out

Date: _______________________

Child's Name	Emergency Phone Number	Contact Name	Time In / Time Out	Signature

Child Daycare Log In/Out

Date: _______________________

Child's Name	Emergency Phone Number	Contact Name	Time In / Time Out	Signature

Child Daycare Log In/Out

Date: _______________________

Child's Name	Emergency Phone Number	Contact Name	Time In / Time Out	Signature